CUT & ASSEMBLE
A CRUSADER CASTLE
IN FULL COLOR

THE KRAK DES CHEVALIERS IN SYRIA

A.G. SMITH

Dover Publications, Inc., New York

For ANTON, a castle builder

Published in Canada by General Publishing Company, Ltd., 30 Lesmill Road, Don Mills, Toronto, Ontario.
Published in the United Kingdom by Constable and Company, Ltd.

Cut & Assemble a Crusader Castle in Full Color: The Krak des Chevaliers in Syria
is a new work, first published by Dover Publications, Inc., in 1986.

International Standard Book Number: 0-486-25200-0

Manufactured in the United States of America
Dover Publications, Inc., 31 East 2nd Street, Mineola, N.Y. 11501

Introduction & Instructions

THE CASTLE

This model of the Krak des Chevaliers was based on French archaeological studies of the late 1920s and early 1930s. The castle, built on a precipice in Syria by the Knights Hospitallers, remains in an excellent state of preservation today. Much overbuilding by local villagers has occurred in past centuries, but most of these structures have been removed. I have attempted to depict Krak as it would have appeared at the height of its development—ca. 1250. While some structures have been simplified for easier construction (the ramps in the inner court, for example), no changes have been made affecting the architectural integrity, strength or function of the castle.

Before constructing your model, read the instructions carefully and become familiar with the individual structures and their positions in relationship to each other.

On the plates, the pieces are labeled by a letter code (such as "TK" for Tower K) and by their number within the structure (such as "TK-3" for the third piece of Tower K). The main pieces of each structure have labels printed on them for easy identification after they have been cut out (these labels will be covered up in the course of assembling the castle).

Following is a checklist of all the structures in this volume, together with their corresponding letter codes, the number of pieces in each structure and the plates on which the pieces are located:

STRUCTURE	LETTER CODE	NO. OF PIECES	PLATE
Walls A–L	—	19	A, B, C, D, E
Towers 1–13	T1	9	F
	T2	2	G
	T3	2	F
	T4	2	F
	T5	4	C
	T6	4	D
	T7	7	H
	T8	4	G
	T9	4	G
	T10	6	G

STRUCTURE	LETTER CODE	NO. OF PIECES	PLATE
	T11	3	H
	T12	4	A
	T13	7	F
Barbican Gate	BG	1	F
Barbican Entrance Ramp	—	1	J
Flags	—	2	A
Ground	G	5	I, J, N
Cistern	—	1	A
Supports (for ground)	—	4	B, E, H
Cross Braces	—	2	C, I
West Glacis	WG	3	J
West Wall K–O	W K–O	1	O
Wall Walk K–O	WW K–O	1	O
South Glacis	SG	2	J
South Wall	SW	6	I, K, L
East Wall	EW	4	M, N
North Wall	NW	4	O
Wall Walk O–P	WW O–P	1	O
Tower H	TH	1	L
Tower I	TI	3	P
Tower J	TJ	3	L
Tower K	TK	4	L
Tower M	TM	2	N
Tower O	TO	2	P
Tower P	TP	2	L
Chapel Tower	CH	3	P
Upper Court	UC	1	M
Upper Court Face	UCF	1	M
Upper Court Ramp	UCR	1	M
Lower Court	LC	1	M
East Wall Ramp	EWR	1	M
Upper Ramp	UR	2	N
Lower Ramp	LR	1	N
Ramp Cover	RC	1	K
Grande Salle	GS	1	K
Upper Hall	UH	1	K

GENERAL DIRECTIONS

For best results in constructing the Krak des Chevaliers these basic tools are recommended: (1) an X-ACTO knife with a #11 blade, (2) a scoring tool, (3) a burnishing tool for applying pressure to glued joints, (4) a straightedge for scoring and cutting, (5) a water-soluble glue, such as Elmer's.

Carefully and accurately cut out all the pieces needed for a given structure. These are numbered and identified by letter codes on the glue tabs. Heavy black lines on the pieces are also cut lines. Never cut out any other areas within a piece unless they are marked with an "X" or the words "Cut out." Some areas so marked are to facilitate gluing; others are for decorative effect. You may or may not wish to cut out the black crenellations in the parapets of the walls and towers.

Broken or dashed lines indicate folds that may not be obvious. For neatest results, score along all fold lines before folding. The towers and walls have parapets which should be scored, folded and glued before the rest of the structure is assembled.

Cut lines that may not be obvious have been noted by the word "Cut." The black lines in the vertical folds of wall and tower parapets should also be cut. Try all parts for fit before gluing.

All glue tabs are indicated with a dot. Apply glue only to the tab itself, never to the receiving surface. Do not apply too much glue—it will seep out and mar the printed surface. Allow each glued joint to dry completely before handling.

Study the assembly diagrams and photographs on the front and back covers to see how the buildings fit together. Be sure to read the special instructions that accompany the diagrams.

The order of assembly is as follows:

(1) Assemble the individual walls and towers of the Outer Ward.

(2) Join the assembled elements of the outer wall. Be sure your working surface is level.

(3) Assemble the ground and supporting structures of the Outer Ward and attach them to the inside of the outer wall.

(4) Assemble the walls and towers of the Inner Ward.

(5) Join the assembled elements of the Inner Ward.

(6) Assemble the Upper and Lower Courts of the Inner Ward and attach them to the edges of the inner wall.

(7) Assemble and attach ramps, stairs and Grande Salle to the inner courtyard.

(8) Assemble the upper and lower portions of the covered entrance ramp and attach the ramp to the East Wall of the Inner Ward.

(9) Apply glue *around* the bottom of walls and glacis of the Inner Ward and attach them to the ground of the Outer Ward.

(10) Attach the ramp of the Barbican Gate and the stairs of the main entrance (Tower 11). Glue flags around toothpicks and attach them to towers.

FINISHING YOUR MODEL

You may wish to color the white edges of the folds along the parapets with colored pencils. Our model on the cover was landscaped using layers of Styrofoam to build up the surface. It was finished with sawdust and sand applied with a solution of 50% water and 50% Elmer's Glue.

The parts of the castle

Tower 8

Wall G

Wall H

Tower 9

Tower M (atop Lower Ramp)

G-4

Tower J

SW-6

Tower K

Cistern

South Glacis

G-5

Tower 7

Wall F

Tower 6

Wall E

Tower 5

Tower I

Wall I

South Wall

Upper Court Ramp

West Wall K–O

Wall Walk K–O

South Glacis

West Glacis WG-3

Wall D

Tower 4

Lower Ramp

Ramp Cover

Upper Court

Upper Court Face

G-1

Wall C

Tower 10

Tower H

East Wall Ramp

Grande Salle

Upper Hall

Tower O

Wall Walk O–P

West Glacis WG-2

Tower 3

Upper Ramp

Wall J

East Wall

Lower Court

Tower 11

G-3

Chapel Tower

North Wall

Tower P

WG-1

Wall B

Wall K

Barbican Gate

G-2

Tower 2

Tower 12

Barbican Entrance Ramp

Tower 13

Wall L

Tower 1

Wall A

5

Standard wall construction

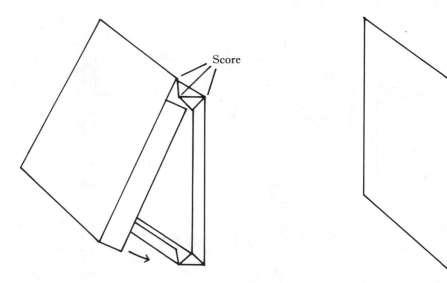

Score

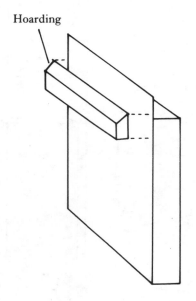

Hoarding

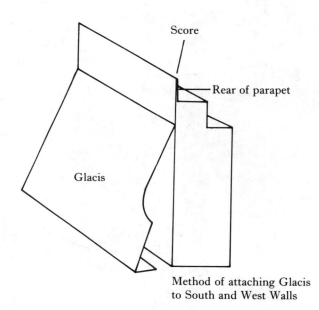

Score

Rear of parapet

Glacis

Method of attaching Glacis
to South and West Walls

Text continues after Plates

6

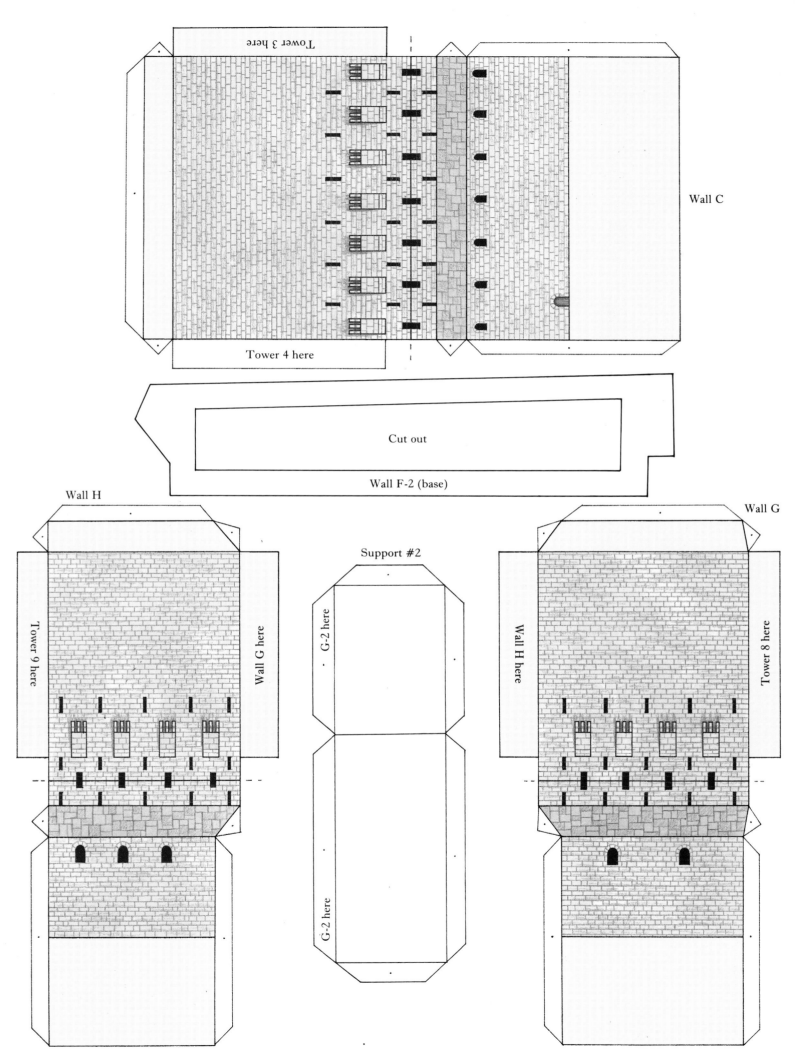

Wall C

Tower 3 here

Tower 4 here

Cut out

Wall F-2 (base)

Wall H

Wall G

Support #2

Tower 9 here

Wall G here

Tower 3 here

G-2 here

Wall H here

Tower 8 here

G-2 here

Plate B

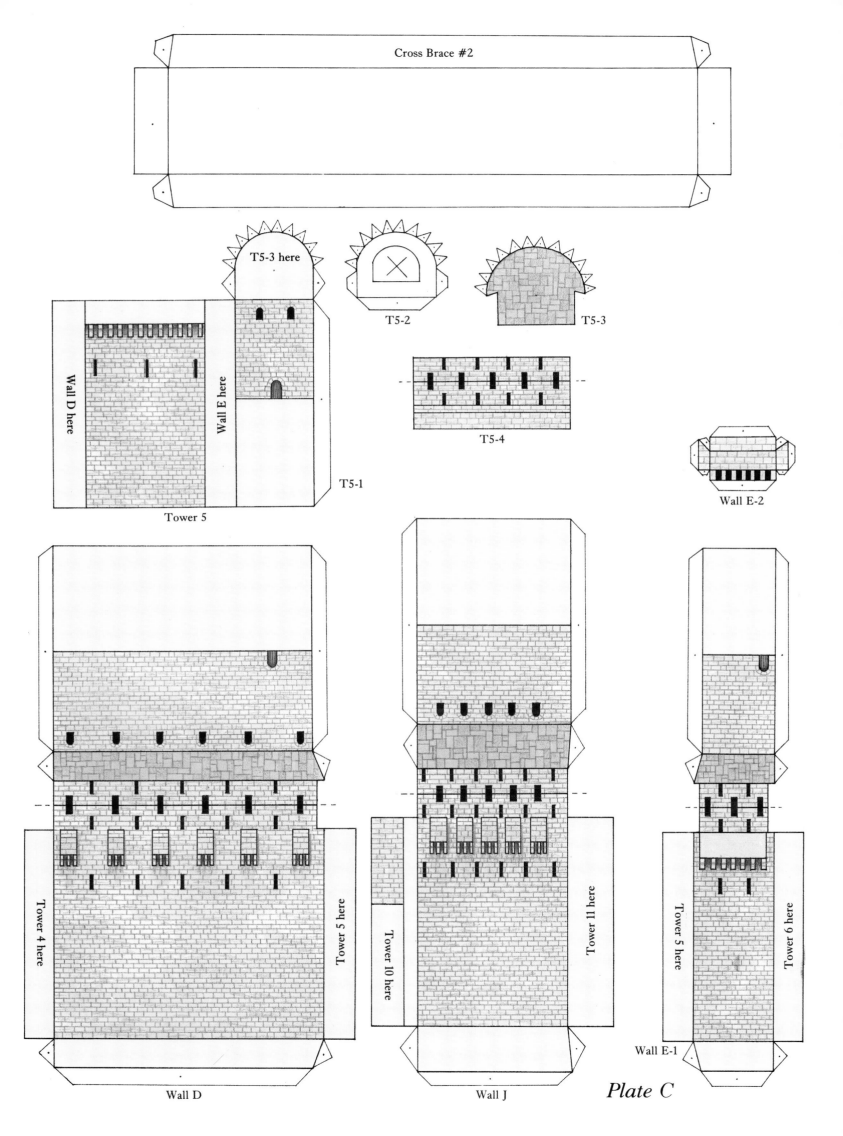

Cross Brace #2

T5-3 here

T5-2

T5-3

Wall D here

Wall E here

T5-4

T5-1

Tower 5

Wall E-2

Tower 4 here

Tower 5 here

Tower 10 here

Tower 11 here

Tower 5 here

Tower 6 here

Wall E-1

Wall D

Wall J

Plate C

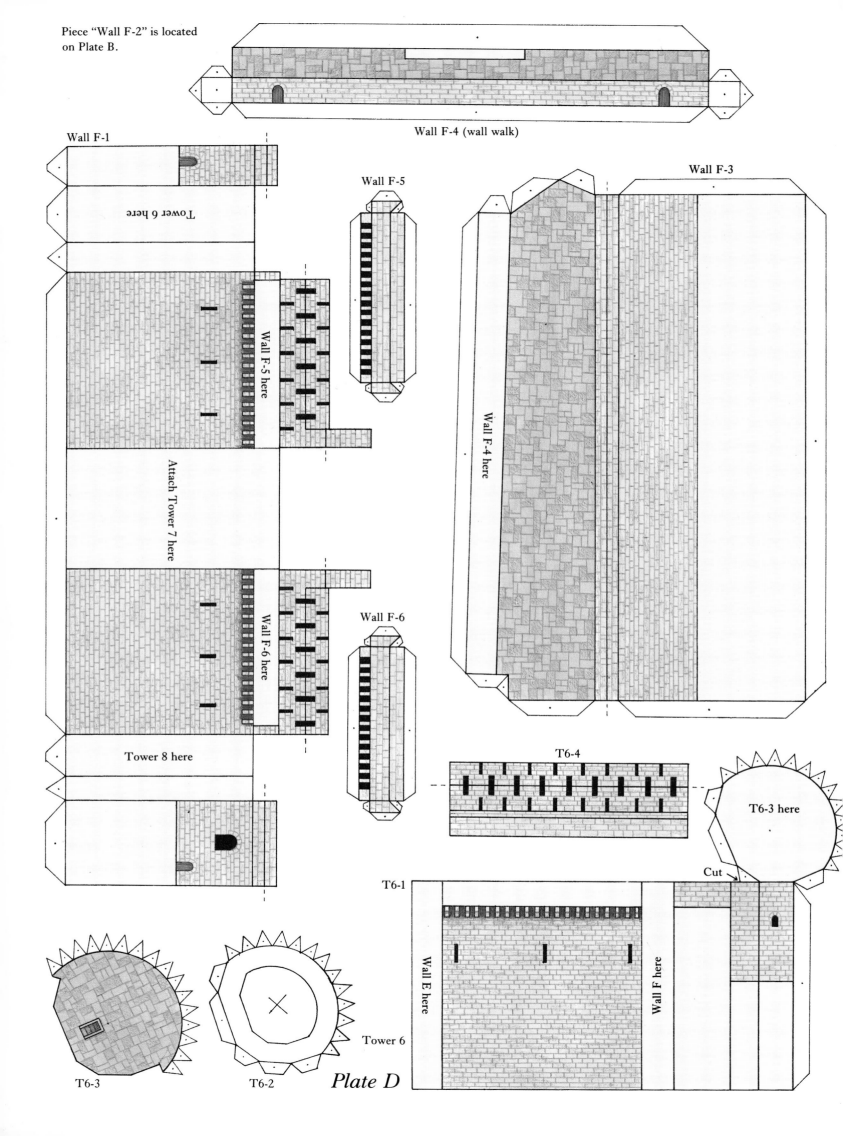

Piece "Wall F-2" is located
on Plate B.

Wall F-4 (wall walk)

Wall F-1

Tower 6 here

Wall F-5

Wall F-3

Wall F-5 here

Attach Tower 7 here

Wall F-4 here

Wall F-6 here

Wall F-6

Tower 8 here

T6-4

T6-3 here

Cut

T6-1

Wall E here

Wall F here

T6-3

T6-2

Tower 6

Plate D

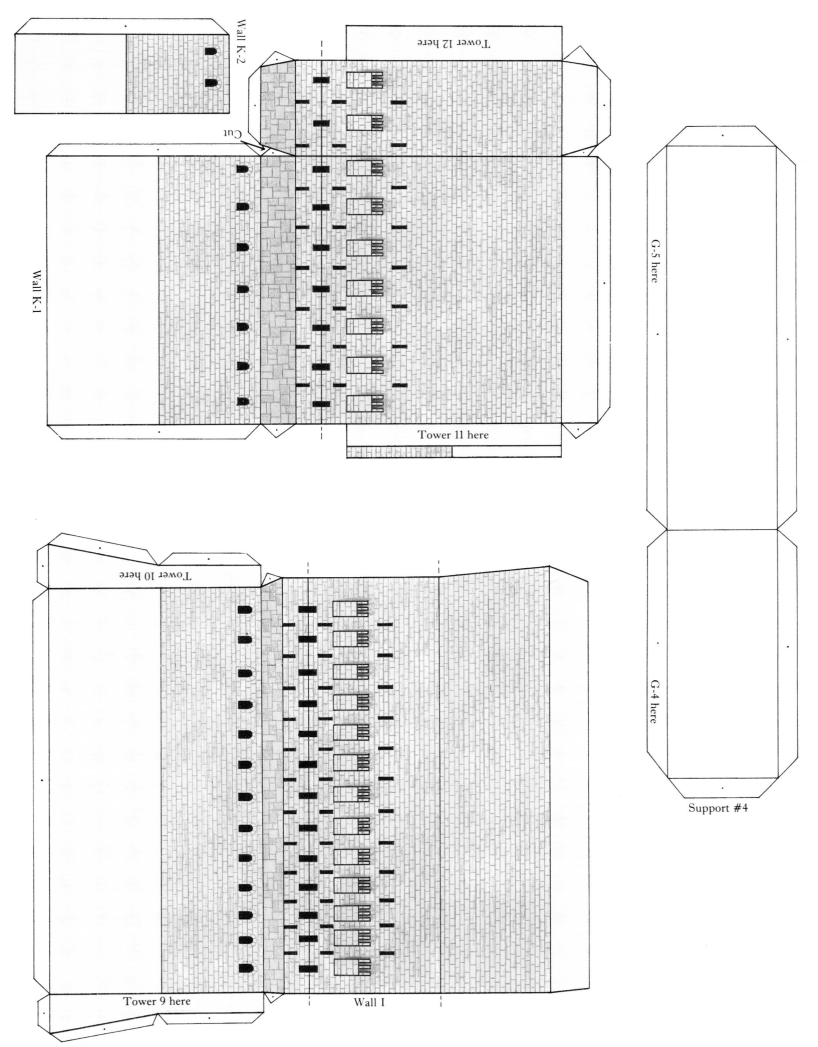

Wall K-2

Wall K-1

Cut

Tower 12 here

Tower 11 here

G-5 here

G-4 here

Support #4

Tower 10 here

Tower 9 here

Wall I

Plate E

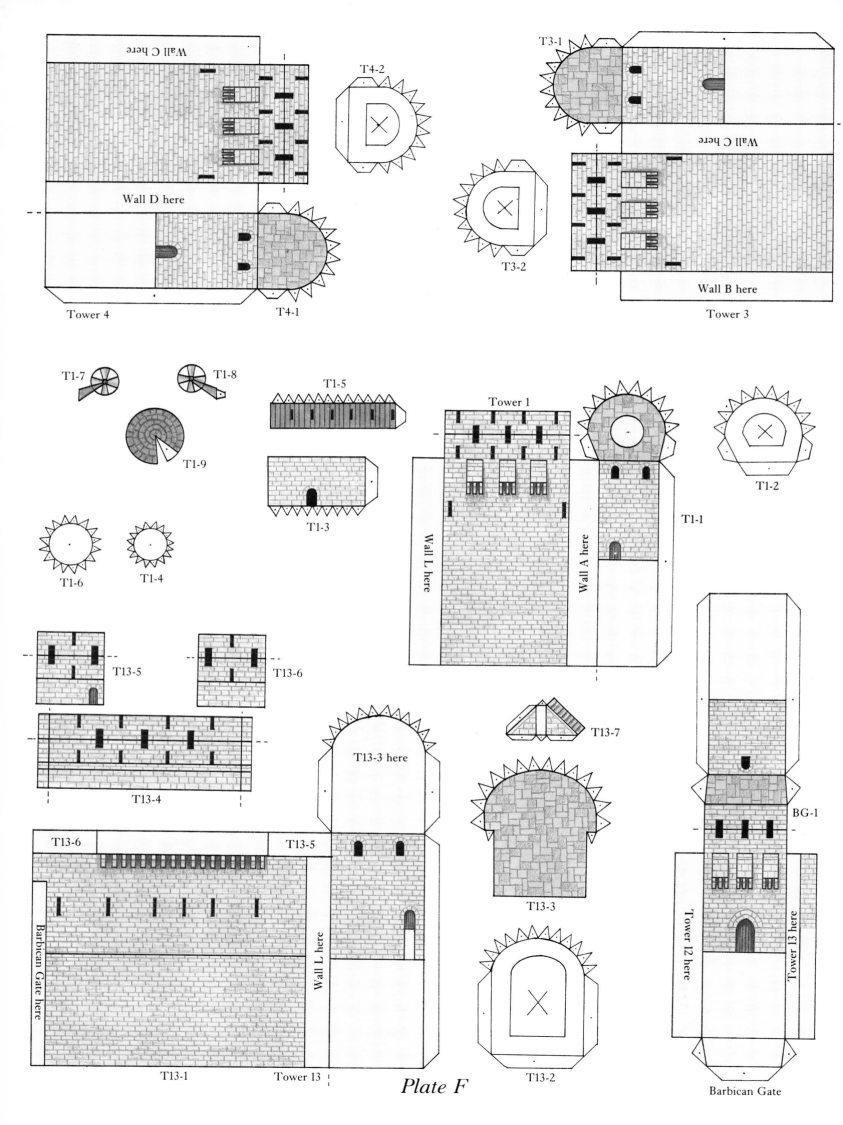

Plate F

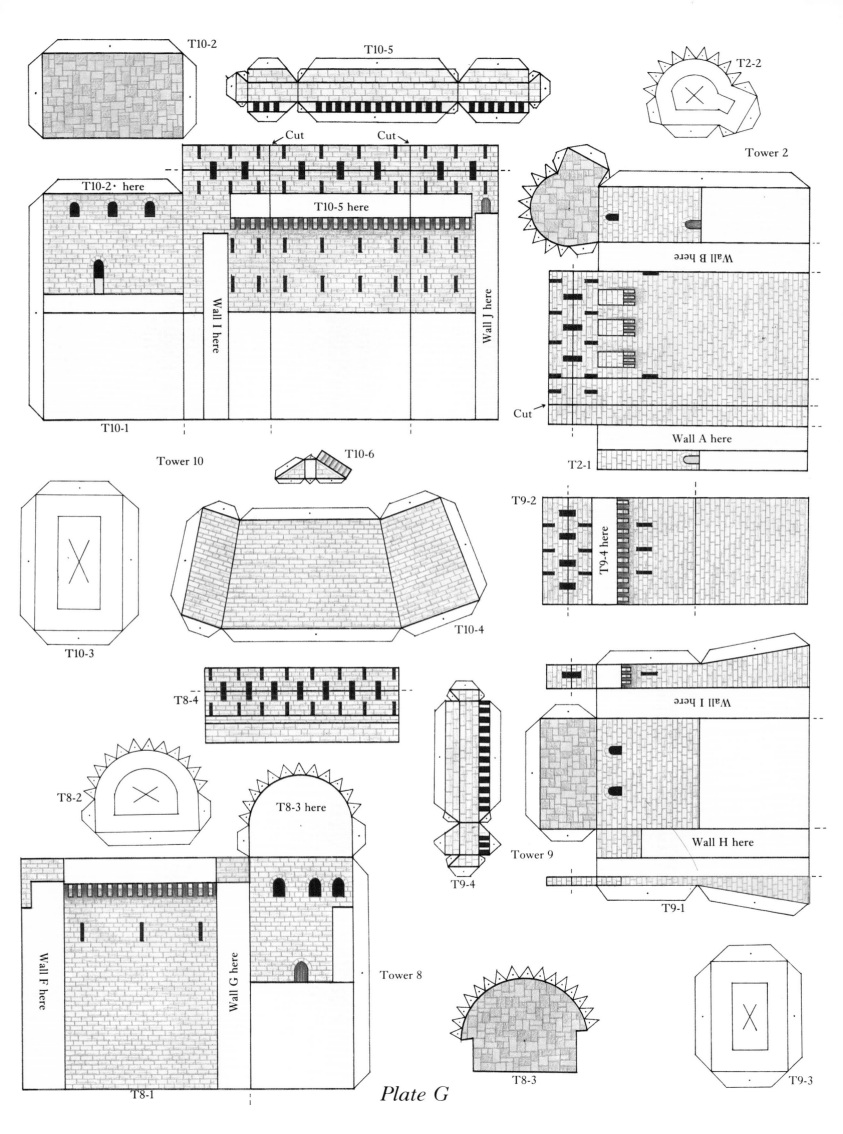

T10-2

T10-5

T2-2

Tower 2

Cut   Cut

T10-2 here

T10-5 here

Wall I here

Wall J here

Wall B here

Cut

Wall A here

T10-1

T2-1

Tower 10

T10-6

T9-2

T9-4 here

T10-3

T10-4

Wall I here

T8-4

T8-2

T8-3 here

Wall H here

Tower 9

T9-4

T9-1

Wall F here

Wall G here

Tower 8

T8-1

T8-3

T9-3

Plate G

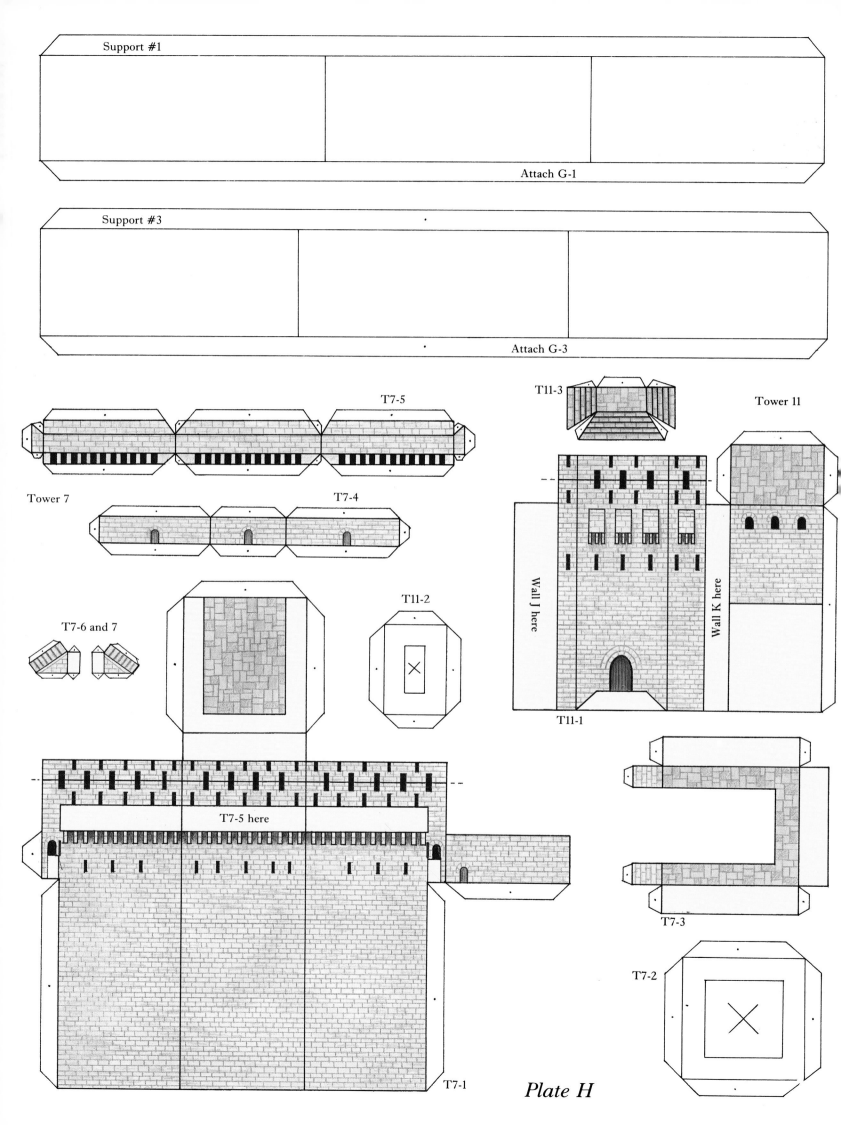

Support #1

Attach G-1

Support #3

Attach G-3

T7-5

Tower 7

T7-4

T7-6 and 7

T11-2

T11-3

Tower 11

Wall J here

Wall K here

T11-1

T7-5 here

T7-3

T7-2

T7-1

Plate H

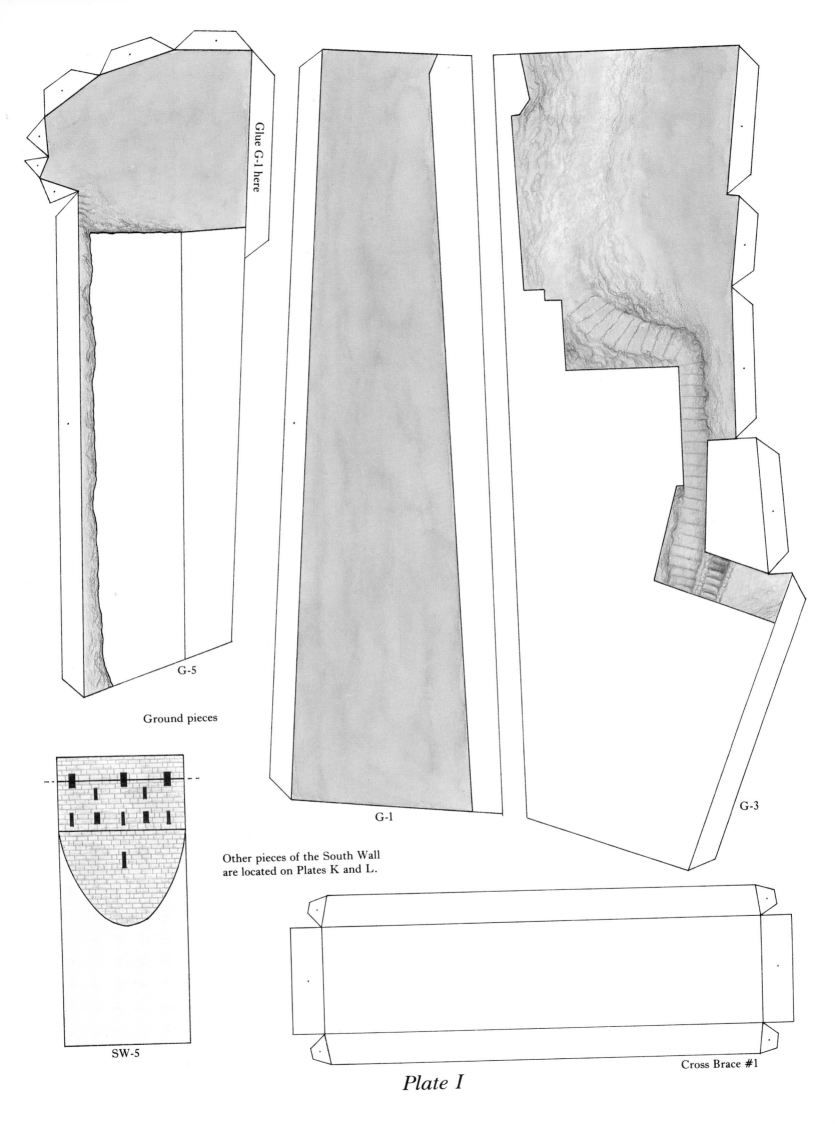

Glue G-1 here

G-5

Ground pieces

G-1

Other pieces of the South Wall
are located on Plates K and L.

G-3

SW-5

Cross Brace #1

Plate I

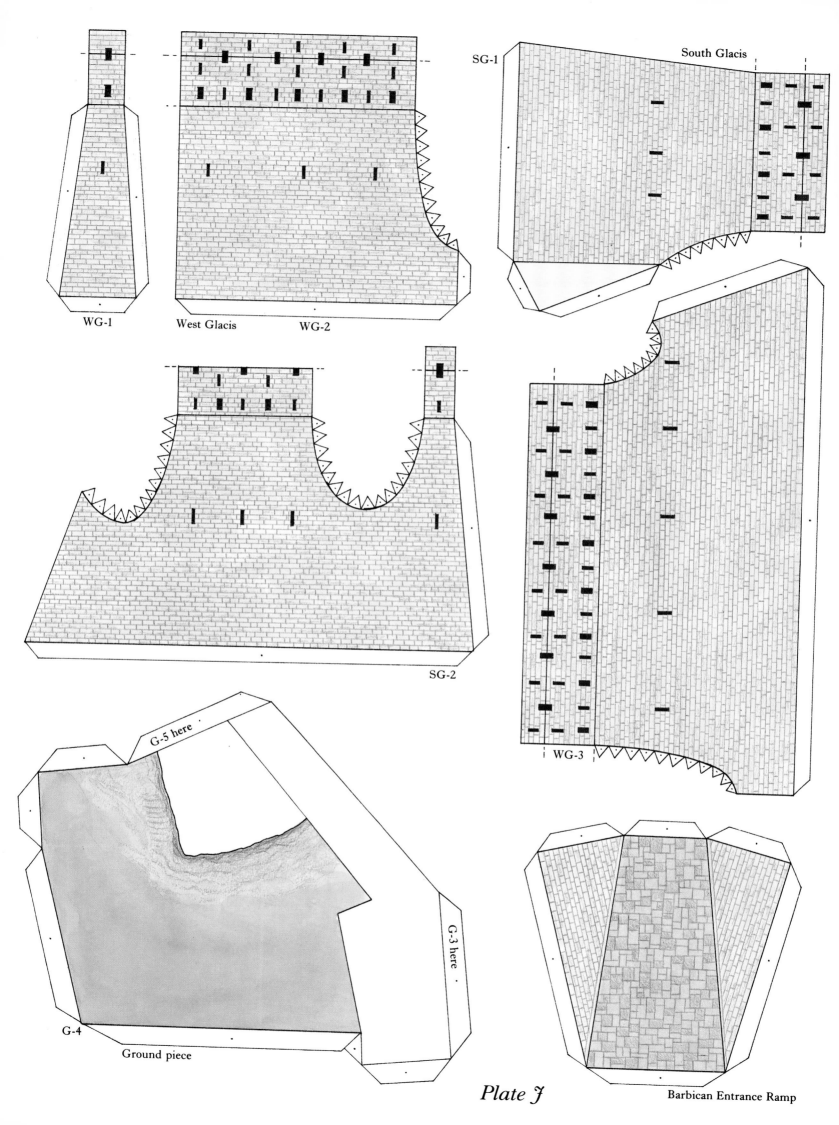

WG-1

West Glacis   WG-2

SG-1   South Glacis

SG-2

G-5 here

G-4   G-3 here

Ground piece

WG-3

Plate J

Barbican Entrance Ramp

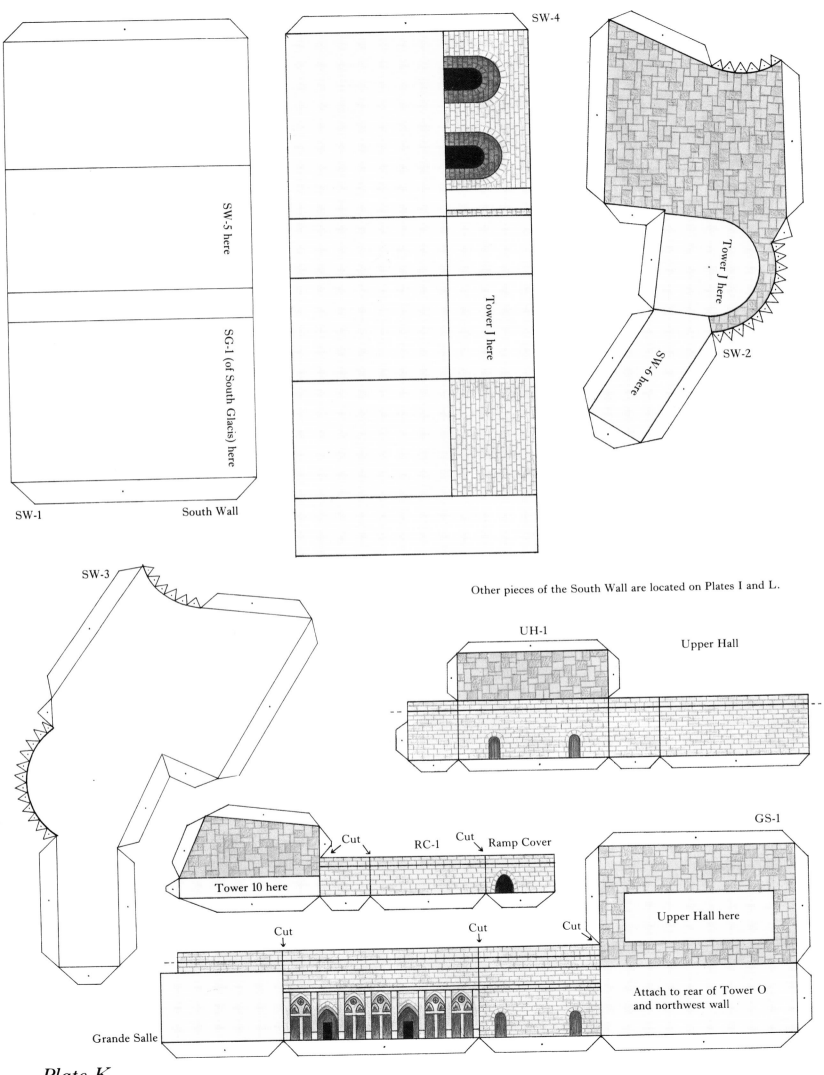

SW-4

SW-5 here

SG-1 (of South Glacis) here

SW-1

South Wall

Tower J here

Tower J here

SW-2

SW-6 here

SW-3

Other pieces of the South Wall are located on Plates I and L.

UH-1

Upper Hall

Tower 10 here

Cut

RC-1

Cut

Ramp Cover

GS-1

Upper Hall here

Cut

Cut

Cut

Attach to rear of Tower O
and northwest wall

Grande Salle

Plate K

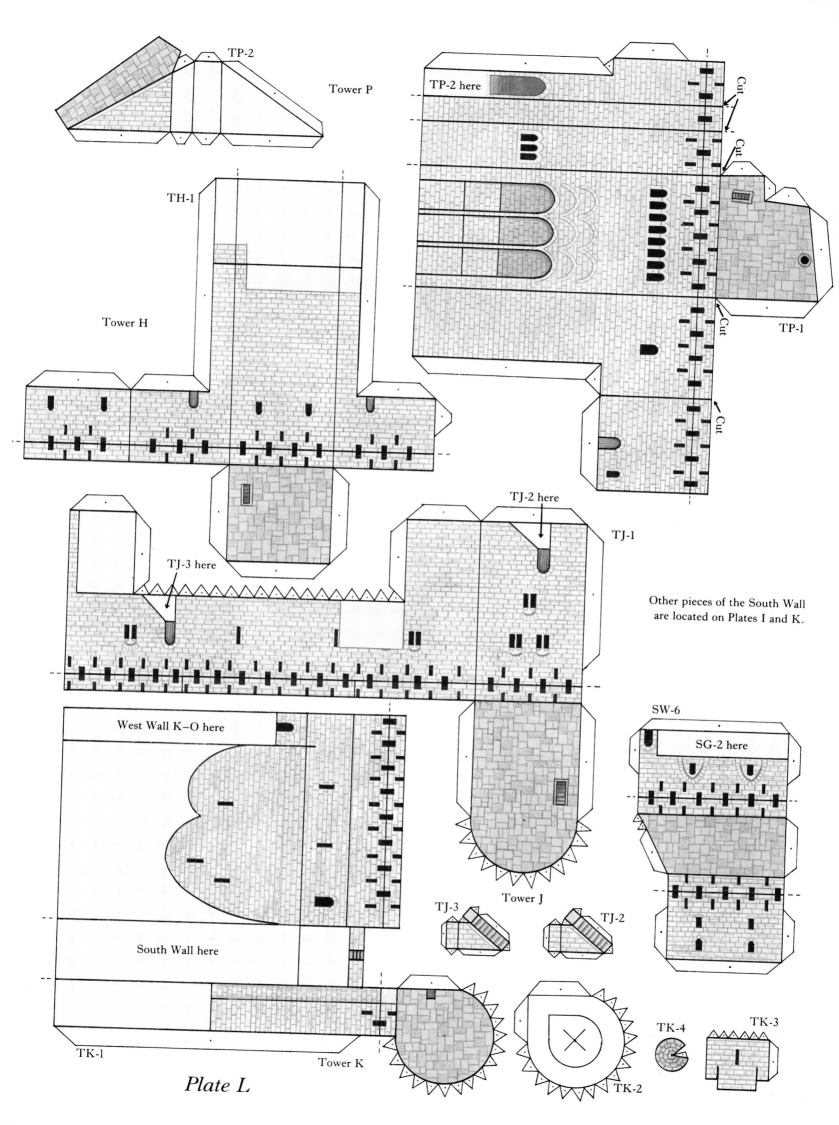

TP-2

Tower P

TP-2 here

Cut

Cut

Cut

Cut

Cut

TP-1

TH-1

Tower H

TP-2 here

TJ-2 here

TJ-1

TJ-3 here

Other pieces of the South Wall
are located on Plates I and K.

SW-6

West Wall K–O here

SG-2 here

Tower J

South Wall here

TJ-3

TJ-2

TK-1

Tower K

TK-4

TK-3

TK-2

Plate L

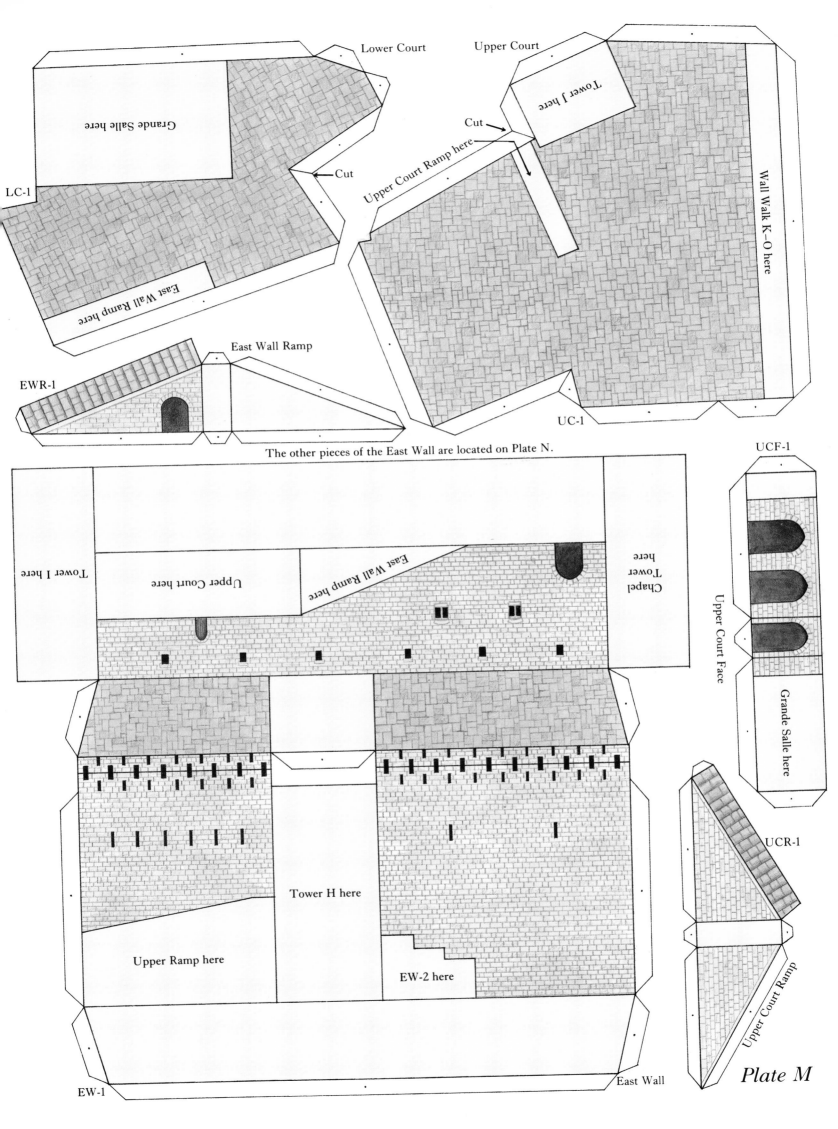

Lower Court   Upper Court

Tower J here

Grande Salle here

Cut

Upper Court Ramp here

Cut

LC-1

East Wall Ramp here

Wall Walk K–O here

East Wall Ramp

EWR-1

UC-1

UCF-1

The other pieces of the East Wall are located on Plate N.

Tower I here

Upper Court here

East Wall Ramp here

Chapel Tower here

Upper Court Face

Grande Salle here

Tower H here

Upper Ramp here

EW-2 here

UCR-1

Upper Court Ramp

EW-1

East Wall

Plate M

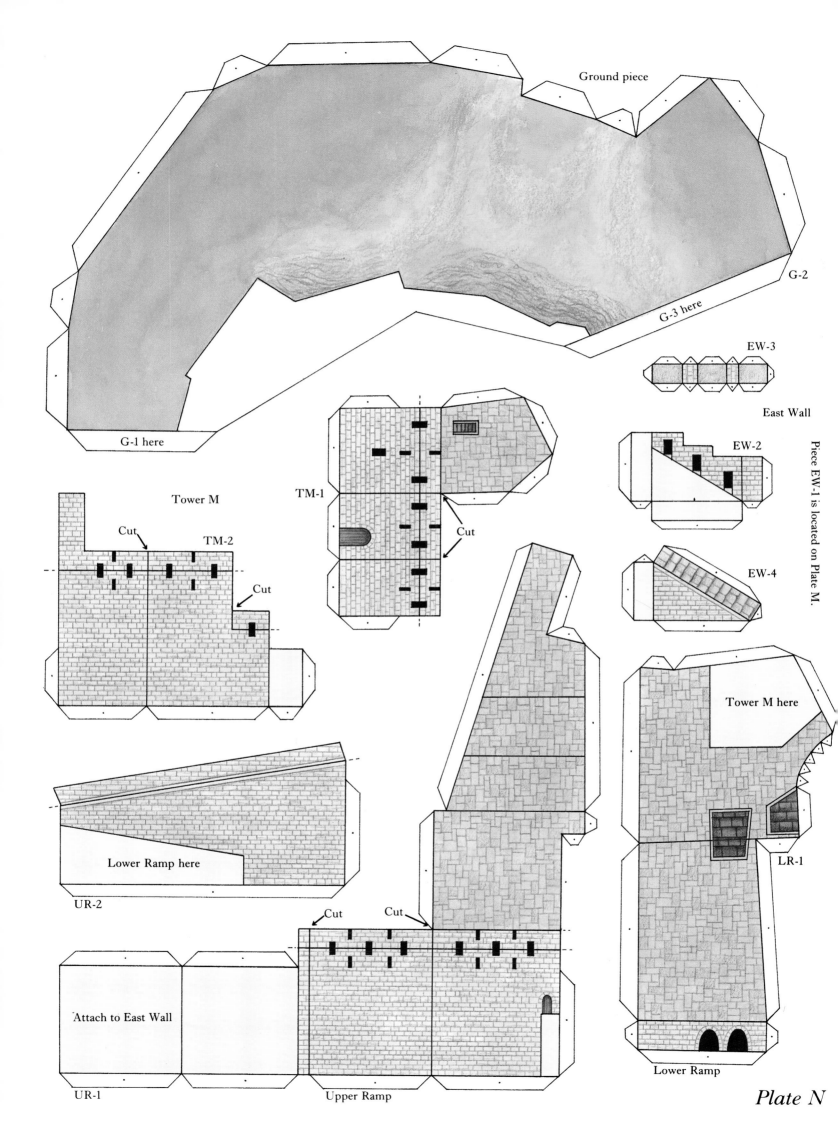

Ground piece

G-2

G-3 here

EW-3

East Wall

G-1 here

EW-2

Tower M

TM-1

Cut

Piece EW-1 is located on Plate M.

Cut

TM-2

Cut

Cut

EW-4

Tower M here

Lower Ramp here

LR-1

UR-2

Cut   Cut

Attach to East Wall

Lower Ramp

UR-1

Upper Ramp

Plate N

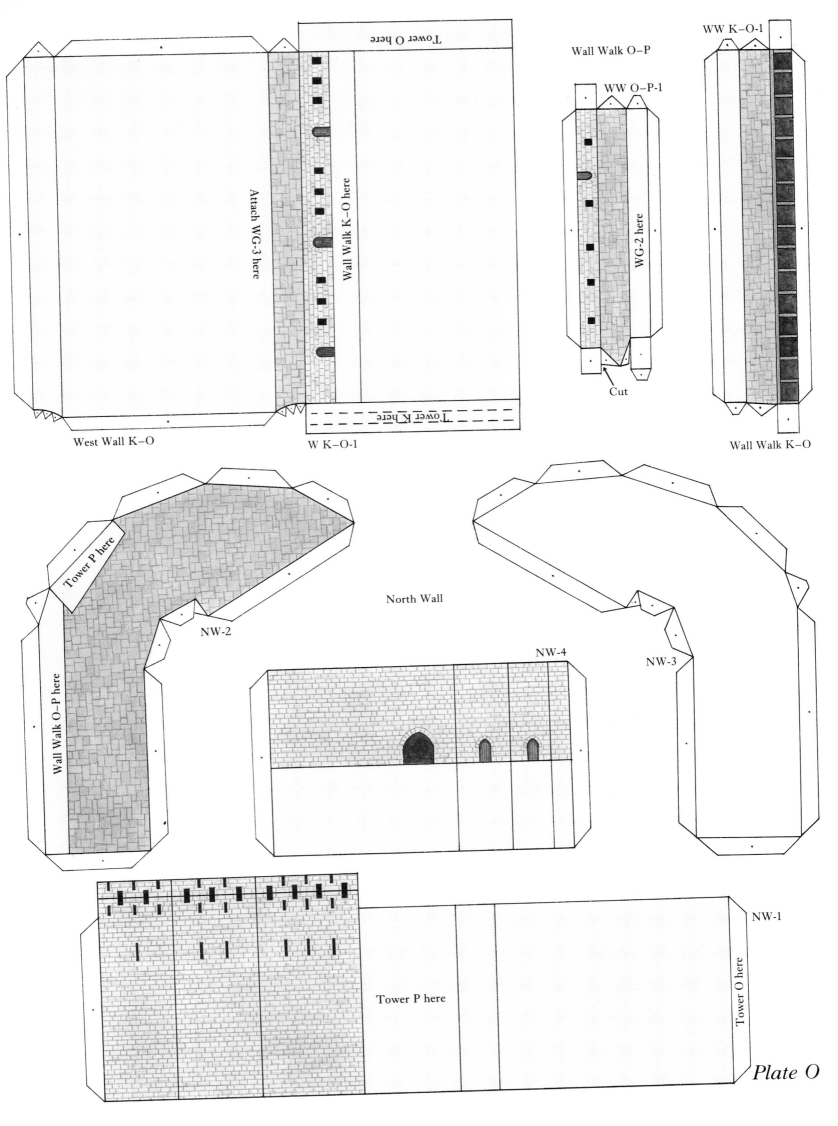

Tower O here

WW K–O-1

Wall Walk O–P

WW O–P-1

Attach WG-3 here

Wall Walk K–O here

WG-2 here

Cut

West Wall K–O

Tower K here

W K–O-1

Wall Walk K–O

Tower P here

Wall Walk O–P here

NW-2

North Wall

NW-4

NW-3

Tower P here

NW-1

Tower O here

Plate O

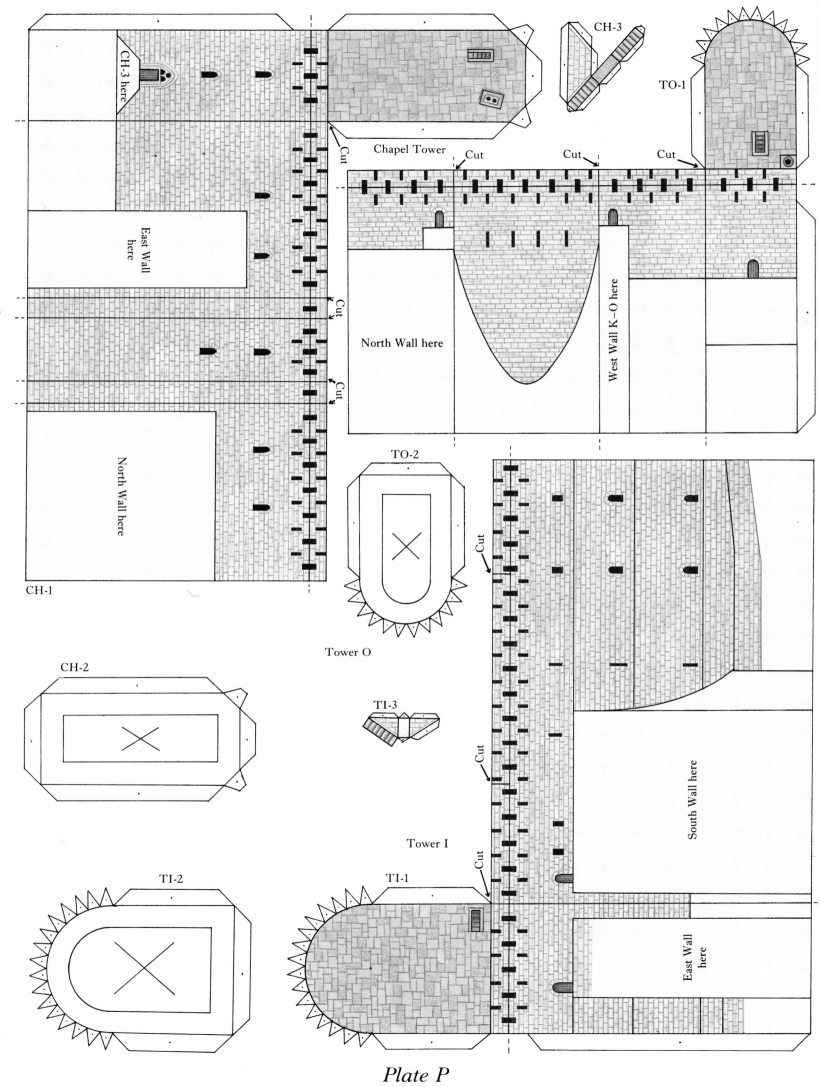

CH-3

TO-1

Chapel Tower

Cut   Cut   Cut   Cut

CH-3 here

East Wall here

North Wall here

West Wall K–O here

Cut

Cut

North Wall here

CH-1

TO-2

Tower O

CH-2

TI-3

Cut

Tower I

Cut

South Wall here

TI-2

TI-1

Cut

East Wall here

Plate P

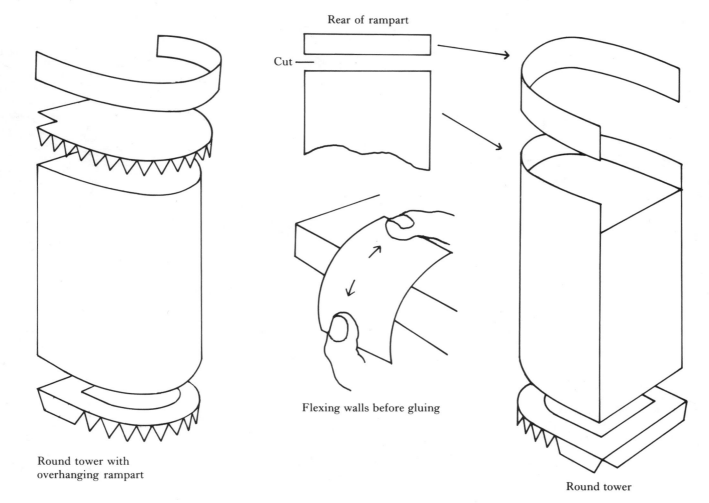

Rear of rampart

Cut

Flexing walls before gluing

Round tower with
overhanging rampart

Round tower

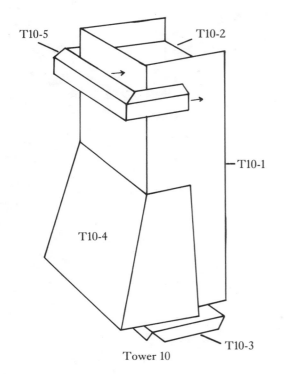

T10-5

T10-2

T10-1

T10-4

T10-3

Tower 10

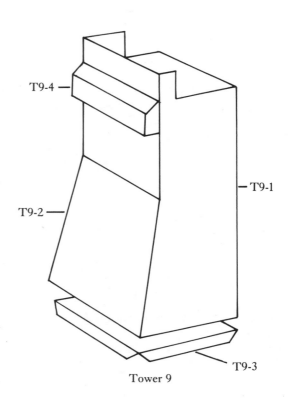

T9-4

T9-1

T9-2

T9-3

Tower 9

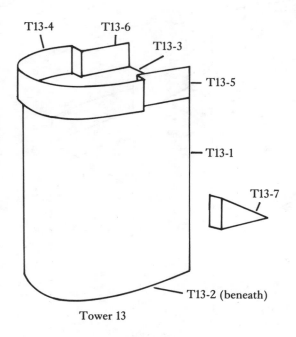

Tower 13

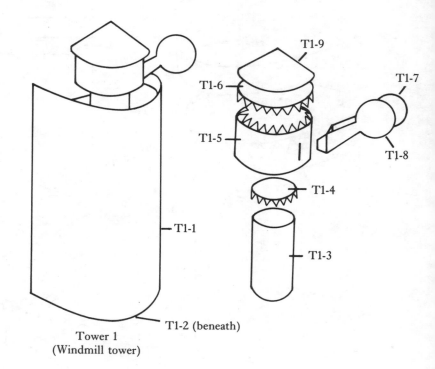

Tower 1
(Windmill tower)

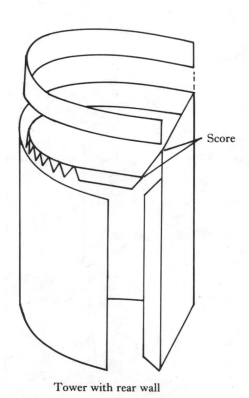

Score

Tower with rear wall

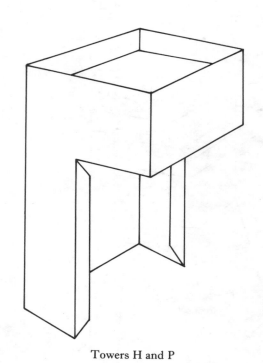

Towers H and P

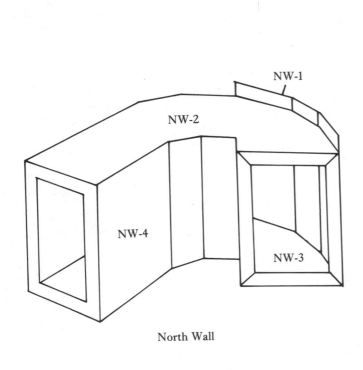

NW-1

NW-2

NW-4

NW-3

North Wall

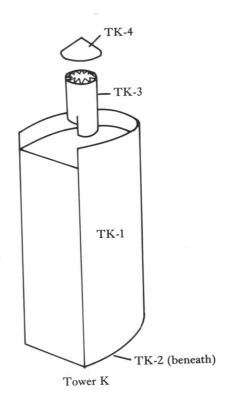

TK-4

TK-3

TK-1

TK-2 (beneath)

Tower K

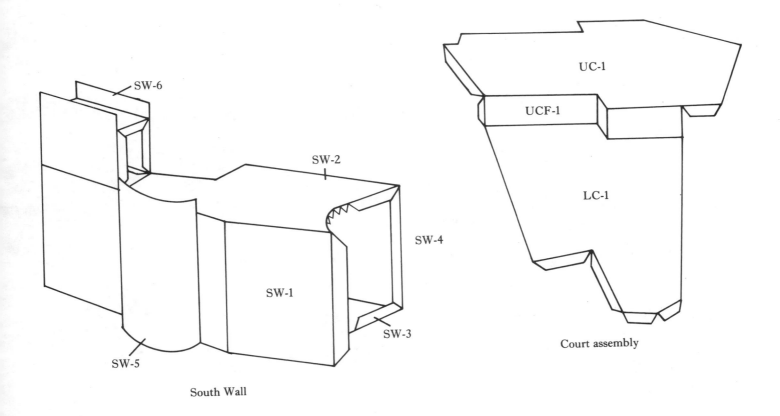

SW-6

SW-2

SW-4

SW-1

SW-3

SW-5

South Wall

UC-1

UCF-1

LC-1

Court assembly

9

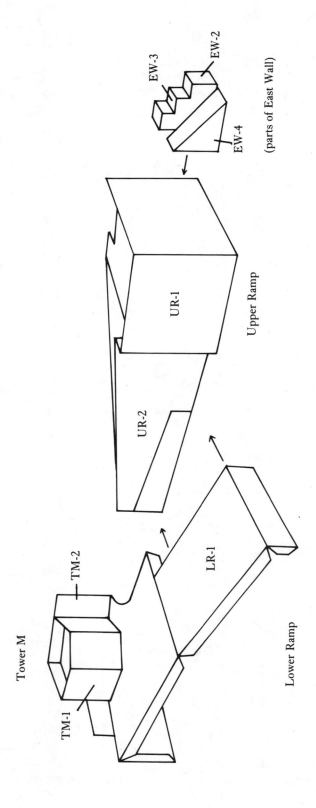

EW-3

EW-2

(parts of East Wall)

EW-4

UR-1

Upper Ramp

UR-2

TM-2

Tower M

TM-1

LR-1

Lower Ramp

10

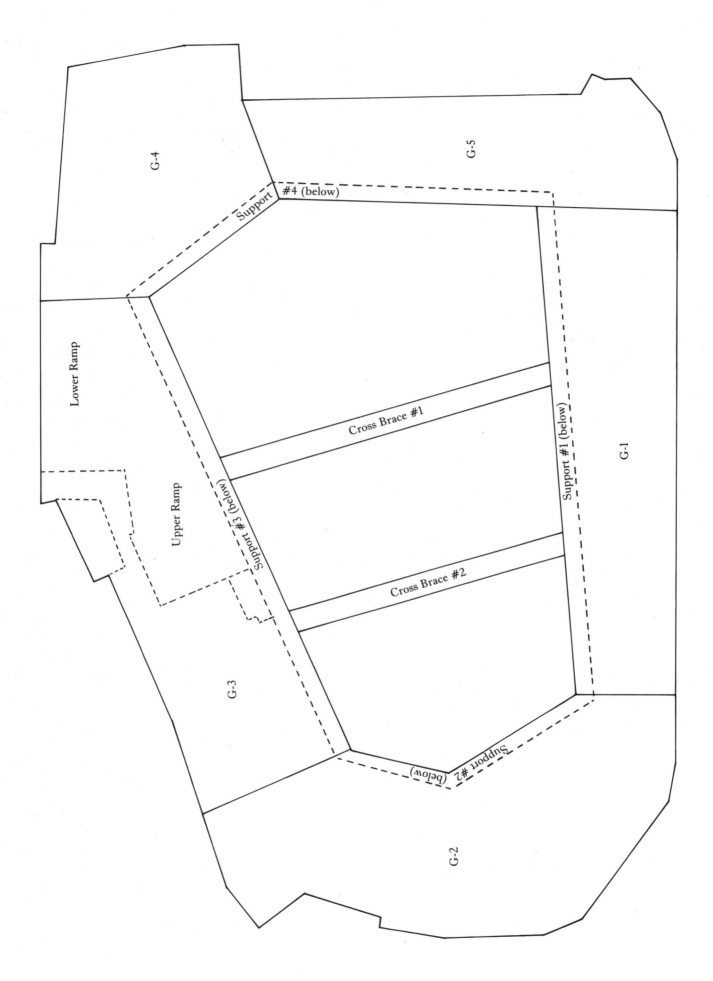

Outer Ward plan

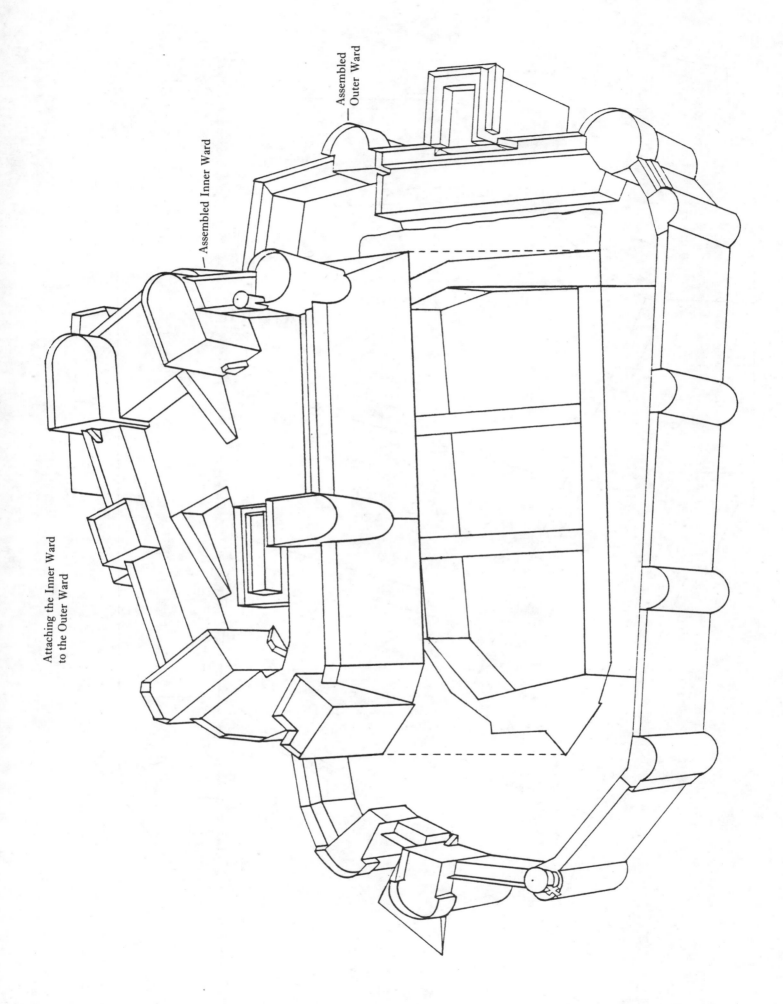

Assembled Outer Ward

Assembled Inner Ward

Attaching the Inner Ward
to the Outer Ward

Krak des Chevaliers: A Brief History

As the Parthenon is to Greek temples and Chartres to Gothic cathedrals, so is Krak des Chevaliers to medieval castles, the supreme example, one of the great buildings of all times.

—T. S. R. BOASE
(*Castles and Churches of the Crusading Kingdoms*)

The Krak des Chevaliers stands near Syria's northern border with present-day Lebanon, some 2,300 feet above the valley of the Nahr al-Kabīr between Homs and Tripoli. A Muslim fortress in earlier times, it was captured by the Frankish crusader Raymond of St. Gilles in 1099. The Arabs had called it Ḥiṣn-al-Akrad, the Franks dubbed it Le Crat, and by an analogy with the word Kerak, meaning "fortress," it became known as le Krak. The "Chevaliers" were the Knights of St. John, also known as the Hospitallers, Crusaders whom Raymond II established at the castle in 1142. It remained a Christian stronghold in a Muslim land from 1142 until 1271. An immensely important strategic and economic post, accommodating 2,000 men and controlling the fertile valley below, it made the Hospitallers a great landed power.

Its earliest stage of development from a simple fortified courtyard cannot be dated accurately, but William of Crat, its first Christian occupant, probably began its conversion to a highly advanced system of concentric defenses. The plan called for a walled courtyard with vaulted compartments built along the inner walls. Square towers, two at the main entrance to the east and others at the south corners and in the west wall, completed the first phase of construction. In 1170 an earthquake probably damaged much of this edifice. Repairs were effected, and by 1188 Krak was again inviolate.

Over a period of time, the outer enceinte with its projecting semicircular towers was added. This second building stage took place in the late twelfth and early thirteenth centuries, and is marked by the change from bossed stone work to smooth-faced stone. The three great towers along the south front and the water-filled cistern were also added at this time.

In 1271 the Krak des Chevaliers was captured by the Mamlūk sultan Baybars I. It remained an important garrison for the Muslim empire until as late as the nineteenth century, although its inhabitants steadily decreased. In 1933 it was ceded by Syria to France, and today stands empty but still noble, an eloquent reminder of the formidable fortress it once was.